IT'S TIME TO LEARN ABOUT ANGELFISH

It's Time to Learn about Angelfish

Walter the Educator

Silent King Books
A WhichHead Entertainment Imprint

Copyright © 2025 by Walter the Educator

All rights reserved. No part of this book may be reproduced in any manner whatsoever without written per- mission except in the case of brief quotations embodied in critical articles and reviews.

First Printing, 2024

Disclaimer

This book is a literary work; the story is not about specific persons, locations, situations, and/or circumstances unless mentioned in a historical context. Any resemblance to real persons, locations, situations, and/or circumstances is coincidental. This book is for entertainment and informational purposes only. The author and publisher offer this information without warranties expressed or implied. No matter the grounds, neither the author nor the publisher will be accountable for any losses, injuries, or other damages caused by the reader's use of this book. The use of this book acknowledges an understanding and acceptance of this disclaimer.

It's Time to Learn about Angelfish is a collectible early learning book by Walter the Educator suitable for all ages belonging to Walter the Educator's Time to Eat Book Series. Collect more books at WaltertheEducator.com

USE THE EXTRA SPACE TO TAKE NOTES AND DOCUMENT YOUR MEMORIES

ANGELFISH

Deep in waters blue and bright,

It's Time to Learn about
Angelfish

Angelfish swim left and right.

With colors bold and fins so wide,

They glide with grace and dance with pride.

Their bodies shine in hues so grand,

Stripes of yellow, blue, and tan.

Some have spots, some shimmer bright,

They sparkle in the ocean light.

Angelfish are thin and tall,

Not like round fish, no, not at all!

Their fins stretch high, their tails so neat,

They twist and turn with gentle feet.

In coral reefs, they love to hide,

Swimming through the rocks inside.

They nibble plants and tiny treats,

Looking for their favorite eats.

It's Time to Learn about
Angelfish

Some eat algae, some eat shrimp,

They poke around with just a glimpse.

With tiny mouths, they take a bite,

Snacking morning, noon, and night!

Angelfish like to stay in pairs,

They swim together everywhere.

A friendly fish, but strong and bold,

In waters warm, not deep and cold.

Some live in oceans, big and wide,

Some in tanks, where they reside.

In homes and aquariums, bright and clear,

Angelfish bring joy and cheer.

They flap their fins so soft and slow,

Through reefs and plants they love to go.

Their colors help them blend and stay,

It's Time to Learn about
Angelfish

Hiding safely through the day.

A fish so fancy, bright, and sweet,

With patterns bold and looks so neat.

The angelfish is quite a sight,

Gliding softly, pure delight!

So now you know this fish so cool,

It swims with style, it has a rule!

With colors bright and fins so wide,

It's Time to Learn about
Angelfish

The angelfish moves with pride!

ABOUT THE CREATOR

Walter the Educator is one of the pseudonyms for Walter Anderson. Formally educated in Chemistry, Business, and Education, he is an educator, an author, a diverse entrepreneur, and he is the son of a disabled war veteran. "Walter the Educator" shares his time between educating and creating. He holds interests and owns several creative projects that entertain, enlighten, enhance, and educate, hoping to inspire and motivate you. Follow, find new works, and stay up to date with Walter the Educator™ at WaltertheEducator.com

www.ingramcontent.com/pod-product-compliance
Lightning Source LLC
LaVergne TN
LVHW052016060526
838201LV00059B/4060